# 33 Keys To Law School Success

*How To Excel In And After Law School*

**Dale Richardson, Esq.**

ISBN-13: 978-0615916712

The Law Office Of Dale Richardson, LLC

www.Dale-Esq.com

# Dedication

### *James Richardson*

*To my dad, Your memory serves as a guide for my life.*

### *Rajeeni Thomas*

*Your memory inspires me to try to inspire others.*

# About The Author

**Author:**       **Dale L. Richardson, Esq.**

**Admitted:**    2001, Georgia

**Law School:**  University of Virginia, School of Law, J.D., 2001

**College:**       Morgan State University, B.S. Electrical
                          Engineering, 1997

**Website:**      www.Dale-Esq.com

Dale L. Richardson has exemplified leadership and excellence at every level of his academic and professional career. He attended Morgan State University where he graduated magna cum laude in December 1997 with a B.S. in Electrical Engineering. While attending Morgan State University, Attorney Richardson was selected as one of nine students profiled by US Black Engineer Magazine in the article "Top HBCU Technology Students." Additionally, he was a charter member and Vice President of Morgan State University's Tau Beta Pi Engineering Honor Society as well as National Finance Chair for the National Society of Black Engineers, President of the Institute of Electrical and Electronics Engineering, and was selected as a Senator to represent Morgan State University at the Maryland Student Legislature.

Attorney Richardson also co-founded several organizations and programs during his tenure at Morgan State University including the Saturday Academy High School Mentoring Program, the Engineering Peer Mentors Program, and the Engineering Student Organizations Council.

In 2001, Attorney Richardson earned his Juris Doctorate from the University of Virginia School of Law. While in law school, he was inducted in to the prestigious Raven Honor Society during his third year. Attorney Richardson had the honor to serve as President of the Black Law Students Association, Student Bar Association Second and Third Year Class Representative, Section Head of the Peer Advising Program, and President of Students United to Promote Racial Awareness. He was also a member of the Asian Pacific American Law Students Association and the Virginia Society of Law and Technology. Additionally, Attorney Richardson remained committed to the local community by volunteering in the Big Sibling Program with the Action for a Better Living Environment organization.

Attorney Richardson began his professional career in the Intellectual Property Group at Kilpatrick Stockton (now Kilpatrick Townsend & Stockton LLP) in Midtown Atlanta working primarily on patent prosecution and other intellectual property issues.

Attorney Richardson also worked in the Construction and Government Representation group at Johnson and Freeman, LLC where he worked extensively with the City of Atlanta's Hartsfield Development Program. At an estimated cost of over $6 Billion, the Hartsfield Development Program was the largest public works project in the history of the State of Georgia.

In 2005, Attorney Richardson was selected as an inaugural member of Georgia Super Lawyers Rising Stars, an honor bestowed on only 2.5% of the attorneys in the State of Georgia. The Law Offices of Dale Richardson, LLC has also had the honor of being selected and serving as Local Counsel for the NAACP Legal Defense Fund in contesting Fulton County's Motion for Unitary Status. Attorney Richardson continues to practice law as the owner of *The Law Offices of Dale Richardson, LLC which focuses on Accidents, Contracts and DUI Defense*. More information regarding Attorney Richardson and his law practice can be found at **www.Dale-Esq.com**.

# Acknowledgments

I would like to thank the many people who helped me on the journey of writing this book. Afi Johnson-Parris, thank you for taking time out of your busy schedule to review the early drafts of this book. Your contributions and suggestions were invaluable. Lauren Brown, thank you for your extensive edits! Some of which did not make it into this first version of the book. LOL! The remaining edits will, however, make it into the next version of the book. I'm excited when I think about how much better that version will be due to your work. To the many other people who continued to encourage me and ask about the progress of this book, thank you as well. Your enthusiasm helped me make it over many hurdles and writing blocks.

# TABLE OF CONTENTS

## SECTION 1: Building The Foundation For Success

## SECTION 2: Putting In the Work For Success

### SECTION 3: Setting Yourself Up For Success

# PREFACE

There are multiple ways to view success in law school. One way is purely based on grades. Another is a student's ability to obtain a job upon graduation. However, consider taking a holistic view of what law school success can be. Each view has its merits. Yet, by using the holistic approach, law school becomes about scholarship, growing as a professional, preparation, networking, learning and enjoying the process. That way, you are fully prepared for your future career as an attorney. Law school grades and future job prospects are a minuscule portion of what true law school success entails. A law student singularly focused on grades will miss out on a wealth of social and professional growth opportunities certain to enhance your overall academic experience.

Keep the big picture in mind. After law school most students intend to practice as attorneys. Accordingly, law school success should include a combination of academic achievement, personal, cultural and business development with an eye toward laying the groundwork for a fruitful career as an attorney for years to come. As a first year student, prepare to expand your scope beyond grades. This will enable you to be better prepared to endure bad use of your scarce time and resources, sleepless nights studying, mind numbing confusion after being taught by the Socratic method, organizational meetings that spin out of control, and daily preparation for classes. Focusing on more than grades will make the difficult times much easier to deal with when you know it is all part of what is required to refine you into a successful attorney.

There will be times you are so focused on the small daily tasks of law school that it is easy to forget the bigger picture. Remember Danielson, in Karate Kid? He was tired of hearing "wax on, wax off." You will be Danielson. You will tire of studying, reading, briefing cases, analyzing rulings, writing papers and memorandums, outlining for exams and attending classes in law school. However, the wax on wax off exercise proved more valuable than Danielson could have imagined. Every event, emotion, and up and down of your life will affect your view of and performance in law school. Refuse to get so caught up in the law school grind that you stop living your life. You will make numerous sacrifices in order to be a successful law student. However, burying yourself in your books and ignoring the world for three years isn't the way to do it. The best law students find a way to balance their workload with their social lives and outside activities. Closing yourself off to the world will lead to you being stressed out and overwhelmed, making you less productive and successful in your law school studies. Perhaps your personality is such that you love to bury yourself into your studies and nothing else. In addition to burning out, you will probably fail to build lasting bonds with your colleagues and miss the myriad of experiences being a law student creates.

*33 Keys to Law School Success* is that holistic approach. It is able to lead you to success in law school while forging the foundation for a promising legal career. **Remember this: The best lawyers are not necessarily the smartest lawyers. The best**

**lawyers are often those who are the best prepared.** Many of the Keys in *33 Keys To Law School Success* will put you in the habit of being better prepared than your peers, while developing skills transferable to arenas other than law school. The skills you gain preparing for class and exams as provided in this book translate into your being prepared for any case or business meeting. Each Key is designed to help you build the skills required to excel in law or any other profession.

Law school can be one of the most rewarding experiences in your life. Follow the *33 Keys to Law School Success* and get the most out of your legal education and career. Following the *33 Keys* will provide you with the framework to succeed in school and beyond.

# SECTION 1

# Building The Foundation

# For Success

# Key #1: Choose The Right School For You

In marriage, choosing the wrong partner means you'll never be as successful as you could have been with the right one. The same is true of law schools. This is often overlooked when anyone discusses law school survival. Law school can be an intense and stressful situation for many people. It's even worse if you don't like your surroundings, classmates, faculty, facility, etc. It's important to take some time to really contemplate what you personally need while in law school.

By no means am I telling you to ignore the legacy, reputation or ranking of any school. On the contrary, I'm suggesting you give careful consideration to ALL factors involved. Here are a few starter questions to ask yourself:

1) How important is it for me to be close to family for support and resources (or far away from the constant distraction of family)?
2) What do the students at this school do other than study?
3) What non-academic organizations are highly publicized and attended?
4) What does the city have to offer? Will city life be too much of a distraction?
5) Will I be able to focus on my work at this school?
6) Does the school offer clinical classes ("clinics") in subjects I might be interested in? (***More on clinics in Key # 31.***)

7) How are the people who look like me treated by the students, faculty, and administration? (women, minorities, disabled, mothers, mature students, etc.)
8) How are the people who think like me treated by the students, faculty, and administration? (religious, conservative, liberal, atheist, extreme, etc.)
9) How cordial are the people who don't look and/or think like me? (We don't have to look or think alike to be great friends or study partners but we do have to respect each other.)
10) What does Alumni participation and interaction look like at the school? Do Alum continue to donate time and money to the school? (Doing so may indicate that the alumni enjoyed their law school experience. Talking to alum of the school can also give you an idea of what they liked or disliked about the school.)

There may be more than one law school that is "right" for you. But you MUST at least identify a few possibilities. Also focus on eliminating the schools that are definitely wrong for you.

One resource law students may find extremely helpful when searching for the right law school is Princeton Review's Law School Rankings. Princeton Review's rankings include such lists as "Best Quality of Life", "Best Classroom Experience", "Most Diverse Faculty", "Best Environment for Minority Students", "Most Competitive Students", etc. Princeton Review is much less focused on irrelevant info like, how many books are in the library. Seriously, who cares? Additionally, it is full of very candid quotes from current students of various law schools.

A second helpful resource was the LSAC (Law School Admission Council). The LSAC offers forums in various locations around the country. The forums often include a law school fair and workshops on topics of interests to incoming law school students such as financial aid and the application process. Many law schools send their reps to the law school fairs to answer questions from prospective students. It's a great place to get preliminary information about several schools at one time. Many schools will send an administrator who works in admissions or financial aid, meaning it can be a good place to make a personal contact at the school.

Once a school feels like it might be a fit, you should definitely visit. Your impressions of the school can completely shift once you set foot on campus. To get a better idea of what a school is like, sit in on a few classes. While you may not understand the material, you'll get a sense of what your own classes might be like and you can compare and contrast it to other schools you visit. Be sure to talk to several students. Ask them about their experiences. What they like and what they hate, maybe even what other schools they considered and why. Be certain to talk to the students outside of those the school administration suggests (of course those students love the school).

For some law students, the advice provided in Key #1 comes a little too late. If that's the case, my advice is the same as folk singer Stephen Stills, "If you can't be with the one you love, love the one you're with."

# Key #2: Be Prepared

Contrary to popular belief, the top lawyers aren't the ones who have the best speaking or argument skills. What makes a great attorney, much like a great boy scout, is always being prepared. The best lawyers are often the ones who are the most prepared.

Typically students enter the preparation phase the summer before law school begins. This is an interesting time. Why? Many of your family and friends will tell you how proud they are of you. Meanwhile you will probably be inundated with horror stories about how difficult law school is, how many times a friend has failed the bar exam, and suggestions of movies you should watch (all of which depict law school as a terrible place to be). Reject the negativity and start getting prepared. Preparing yourself includes resisting the negativity and doing one or more of the following:

1) Intern for a lawyer or a law firm. Working as an intern gives you a sneak peek into what life may be like after law school. You'll get a glimpse into the good, the bad and, sometimes, the ugly of working as an attorney. It also gives you a visual goal that can help motivate you during law school and give you that extra boost during the hard times. It can also help you determine if you'd prefer to work in a large firm, small firm, corporate environment or start your own firm. You can use the bad you see during the summer to steer away from certain firms and help you

narrow down your future job offers. Additionally, it can give you an additional contact to call on for advice during law school and maybe even call on for a summer clerkships after your first year in law school. Remember to keep your summer internship in perspective. Law firm environments and personalities can vary widely, so remember that during and after your summer experience. Not all small or large firms are similar.

2) LSAC Forums, (*mentioned in Key #1*) are great places to get useful information on law school preparation and meet representatives from various law schools. Forums offer workshops on topics like LSAT preparation, the application process, financial aid, etc. Without a doubt, visiting the LSAC Forums is much more beneficial if it occurs prior to your acceptance to law school. However, if you haven't already been, there is still plenty of value in attending the forums the summer prior to law school.

3) Pre law school programs are also a good idea if you can afford it. While costly, their greatest benefit lies in demystifying law school. Attending one of these programs doesn't guarantee law school success (although some will tout that on their website and in their literature), but they do help you develop a few tools to add to your toolbox giving you a significant advantage over your classmates. Just search "law school prep courses" online and you'll see a bunch of options.

4) Nothing. That's right. For some of you, it will be better to just take the summer off and relax. Taking a break might be exactly what you need to get geared up for a long and arduous first year in law school. Make sure you know that you fit into this category or risk wasting an opportunity to get "ahead" of your classmates.

**There is so much to do during law school.** *33 Keys To Law School Success* may have you feeling there is NO WAY you can get it all done, but YOU CAN. Just remember that being prepared should remain at the top of your list. The Keys in *33 Keys To Law School Success* are all about making sure that you are prepared and successful during your law school career. However, there are a couple Keys that I want to emphasize. Here are a few things you should make sure you do during law school:

1) **Read Your Cases and Read Them BEFORE Class.** Some people will tell you to save time and read the commercial briefs (shortened outlines of the cases keyed to your particular case book) or briefs that were created by other students who previously used the same book. **This is not good advice and you should ignore it.** Commercial briefs are SUPPLEMENTS to be used in a pinch. They are also great for reviewing after you read to make sure you noticed the important aspects of the case. However, there is NO SUBSTITUTION for reading the actual case. As time consuming and arduous as this seems at first, it does become easier with time. The more you read cases, the faster you'll become at reading them and the faster you'll

get at accurately spotting the important information within the cases.

2) **Brief Your Cases BEFORE Class.** Just like reading cases, you'll get better at it the more you do it. It will also make preparing for and studying for exams a lot easier if you have already briefed your cases during the semester. (For examples of case briefs, glance at the commercially prepared case briefs sold in your law school book store.) Being prepared for class allows you to better understand what is happening in class. There are days when you will be utterly confused. Minimize this feeling by reading and briefing your cases prior to class. If you don't read and brief the cases, you'll be spending precious class time trying to figure out what's important and what's not. Instead of adding to your brief, you'll be taking notes. Most law students frantically copy everything that's said "just in case" it's important. If you brief cases beforehand, you'll be able to listening "actively" *(See Key #11)* instead of writing down everything that's said.

3) **Read the Keys in *33 Keys To Law School Success.*** It's a shameless, but relevant plug. I wouldn't have written this book if I didn't think the information was valuable and useful. Do more than just skim the titles of the chapters. Actually READ EACH CHAPTER. Every law student is different so you never know which Key will be the one that helps YOU the most.

# Key #3: Get To Know
# Your Professors

Professors are people too. Okay maybe they aren't but let's act like they are for a minute. (Just kidding!) The reality is your professors are the top scholars in the areas of law they research or practice. Many of your professors literally wrote the book on the subject matter they are teaching. So we can debate whether or not they are people but there is no debate that your professors generally know what they are talking about.

Some schools promote and encourage student/professor interaction. Some schools offer take a professor to lunch programs where the school will reimburse you for the professor's lunch if a group of students take her or him to lunch. However, if your school doesn't do anything to facilitate the relationship, that doesn't mean you can't take the initiative yourself. Law school professors will see you as more of an adult than your undergraduate professors may have. So while they may seem to have a certain air of authority in class, they are often open and inviting of any student who actually takes an interest in learning more about who they are and what they do. Visit all of your professors at least once during office hours. Always go with a substantive question, but don't be afraid to ask about other topics that come to mind or flow from the conversation. If you notice an interesting photo or book in the professor's office, ask about it.

Start out by trying to like your professors. It may not always be possible. Still, there's something about liking a professor that makes you want to work harder for him or her. If your office visit solidifies your dislike of your professor, oh well, you tried. Professors are worth building relationships with as they often hire assistants during the summer to help them research various issues for articles or books they are in the process of writing. You may possibly need references from your law professors when you apply for jobs or maybe even your bar license. It helps to know a few professors on a personal level, before you need them to write a recommendation for you. There is nothing worse than reintroducing yourself seconds before asking for a recommendation. No one wants to start off a recommendation request with, "You may not remember me but..."

Another great thing about professors is, as I said earlier, they are often the leaders, experts or trendsetters in the area(s) of law that they teach. There is nothing better than being able to call a former professor and expert to help you through difficult issues you may encounter as a practicing lawyer. For Free.

# Key #4: Dance With The Date That Got You There

Chances are, you did something right in school to end up getting admitted into a law school (or you have wealthy parents which works too). Often, the sheer amount of work, the Socratic method, the fact that your grade is based on a single exam at the end of the semester... whatever the reason, many people adopt different study habits in law school. **Do not do this.** I'm talking about your style of study. Figure out how you learn best. Be sure to find ways to incorporate the most effective study habits from undergrad into your law school study routine. For example, did you study best with flashcards? What about using flowcharts? Did you study better in the morning, evening or night? Did you study best when you reviewed the material by yourself first followed by a study group? Did you learn better when you were tutoring your peers? Whatever your successful undergraduate habits were, bring them with you to law school.

Also, it's important to try new methods of studying as well. Don't abandon your tried and true methods, but be willing to try out a few new study techniques. You may find another option to add to your mainstay of study habits.

Understand "how" you learn. For example, many engineering students learn through the repetition of working problems. There are no "problems" to solve in law school BUT don't overlook that you have proven that you are used to learning through repetition.

Maybe you can develop a means of repetition such as creating flash cards or listening to recorded lectures over and over.

What environment works best for you? Do you work best in a bustling café or bookstore? Do you need the complete silence of a library or empty house? Do you absorb more when you are by yourself or when you have someone to bounce questions off of? Put serious thought into how you study best and incorporate your most successful past habits with new study skills to develop an effective study routine.

# Key #5: Exercise And Pray
# Or Meditate

Let's get straight to the point. You won't be doing yourself any favors if you are too sick to go to class. Therefore, it's important that you do what you can to stay healthy during law school (and life for that matter). Part of staying healthy is exercise and a balanced diet. Whether you want to admit it or not, how you feel affects how you perform. How you treat your body affects how you feel. So, you should try to keep your body feeling well. If you are tired all the time, you will retain less information and be less able and willing to stay up to study or finish briefing cases.

It's so easy to pig out on junk food while you are running from class to class or studying during exams. Fight the urge. Junk food doesn't provide the long lasting nourishment you need to keep studying and focused. Now, I am realistic and I know junk and fast food are inevitable for most law students. I'm just saying to mix in healthy food and to include exercise in your weekly routine.

It's also an added bonus that exercise can reduce stress as well. Who's in more need of stress relief than law students? You don't need to become a gym rat. You can commit yourself to walking or jogging several miles a day. You can join a softball or football team that plays and practices weekly. Find rollerblading partners or get a group of friends to work-out to one of those infomercial DVDs. Just do something that insures that you are keeping your body active and fit as well as fighting off the stress of law school.

If you don't already know, your mind, body and soul are all connected. Meaning a healthy body, yields a healthy spirit/soul as well. Whether or not you are religious, find a way to center and calm your spirit. For me, prayer works wonders. Other students may prefer meditation, walking or running amongst nature. Whatever your method, set aside time daily for silence, reflection, focus and recalibration.

In addition to my regular daily prayers, I made it a routine to also pray before every exam. It definitely had the effect of calming me, easing my mind and it gave me the perseverance to push through the exam even when the first question tempted me to immediately "lose my religion." Whether you choose prayer or meditation, or none of the above, work a means of clearing your mind into your daily routine as an additional way to reduce stress and remain centered.

# Key #6: Thinking Like A Lawyer Doesn't Mean Becoming Someone Else

Law school teaches you to "think like a lawyer." That's fine. But don't let that change who you are. Too often, law students begin to change their identity whereby being a lawyer becomes the central focus of who they are. Practicing law should be your profession, not who you are. It is one important component in the overall total package of you.

Being a lawyer is a great and honorable profession. However, when lawyers choose to "act" like the stereotypical lawyer, the greater community redefines our profession as one of opportunistic, self-serving, uncaring, money hungry, etc. There are absolutely attorneys who feed into the stereotype. Don't become one of them.

Thankfully, the great majority of lawyers that I know personally are nothing like the stereotype. Perhaps it's the lawyers I choose to associate with, yet these are professionals who are caring, believe in the importance of treating their clients as people no matter what their circumstances, and understand all lawyers work in a service industry. It should be our primary goal to serve our clients, whom without we would have no industry. Many of the lawyers I know provide competent counsel and advice to clients. Sometimes that means less money for the attorney because the least expensive option is in the best interest of the client. In my experience, lawyers who do what is right and do a good job at it ultimately bring in more money and clients over the long term.

Even amongst my own law school classmates, there were those who felt that becoming a lawyer meant being argumentative, rudely cutting people off and letting them know that what they are talking about isn't relevant or material. These people did their best to add to the belief that lawyers are all "a$$h&!es." I implore you to be a great person first and a great lawyer second. Not only is it good for the profession, it's good for your soul and good karma.

# Key #7: Enjoy The Experience

There are times when this Key may sound like an impossible task during your first year of law school, but it is not. Take the time to make lasting friendships. Not only will it make your law school experience more enjoyable but often these friends become referrals and resources later as a practicing lawyer. Life is too short to become focused on the wrong things. At the end of the day, you are in school to train to become a great lawyer. Law is a profession, not a way of life. It shouldn't define who you are. Stay true to who you are no matter what.

It's easy to get consumed with the everyday struggle of law school. But it helps to keep things in perspective. Remember how excited you were when you found out that you were accepted into law school? Remember all the family and friends who thought you were the smartest thing since Einstein? Remember all of your idealistic plans for the future?

You do have to make sure that you study and get your work done to be successful in law school. But it's equally important to take breaks, to get out and to remember that there is a world outside of law school. It's important to remember that you have interests outside of law. Your sanity is important to being successful in law school. As Dean Scott, former Dean of UVa Law School would often say, "law school is a marathon not a sprint." You don't want to get fatigued too early. It's a long semester. Take your breaks so you don't wear yourself out too early. Don't forget your interests and make sure you are doing things that keep you excited and motivated about life. Plus, a positive attitude can work miracles. Say it with me, "the cup is half full, not half empty"... hopefully with something that makes you smile... responsibly.

Use all the clichés you need to use to keep this concept in your mind. Make sure when you look at things, you see the glass as half full instead of half empty. Don't forget to smell the roses. Life is what you make it. Law school is like a box of chocolate. Look before you leap. Okay I'm not sure that the last two fit, but you get the idea.

*Live, Laugh, Learn* is a good mantra for law students. Your primary focus during law school will be the learning part, but make sure to do all three in copious amounts.

# SECTION 2

# Putting In The Work
# For Success

# Key #8: Learn To Manage Your Time

Time management is extremely important in law school. Law school (and the practice of law) can be very demanding of your time. So it is extremely important that you learn to effectively manage your time. There are endless books, DVDs, courses, etc. on time management. There are just as many ways to accomplish effectively managing your time. The time management techniques that work best for me may not work at all for you. Do a bit of research and a little digging into how to manage your time. Not a morning person? Schedule classes and meetings in the afternoon. Can't avoid morning classes? Figure out a way to make sure you wake up and get to class in time every morning. Take the time to find what works best for you.

Some of the most successful law students seemed to get adequate sleep and have the best time in law school. It's because they knew how to best manage their time, making it possible to enjoy more than the four walls of the library. Managing their time effectively included taking breaks during the day, which allowed them to stay focused and awake during periods of studying. If you know a five-minute break quickly becomes a three-hour break, modify your blocks of study time into big chunks.

There were several students I knew who treated law school like a job. Often these were individuals who had careers before law school. They woke up early whether or not they had an early class and started "working." At the end of the "work" day they would put up their books and relax. Some of those students were done by 6 pm each night. There were exceptions where they had to stay up late to finish an assignment or study for a test, but for the most part, they maintained a consistent routine. I envied those students, and there discipline paid off. Consider if this method could work for you and, if so, do it. It is definitely an effective option for time management.

There were other students who worked best by prioritizing the chores and tasks of the day and working on them where they seemed to fit best. It may often mean later nights, but it also can sometimes mean starting your day later as well. Customize your time planning to your needs; just be sure to create a schedule. Yours may be completely different from other law students, but what matters is that you make enough time to work, study and play. Managing your time well is a critical Key to law school success.

Successful time management almost always includes a task list. Regardless of what works best for you as far as how you organize your day, you must keep a task list. Prioritize what needs to get done and include deadlines. That way, you'll be able to plan ahead for things that can't be moved or that are going to require large amounts of your time. It's not fun to blow off two or three hours of the day and then remember late at night that you never read the cases for Monday's classes. Or realize on Friday that your first draft of your memo is due on Monday after you already planned an exciting weekend or committed to several events, functions or travel over the weekend. A quick glance at your task list each day will help you avoid those situations.

Just make sure you are doing something more than "going with the flow." Be flexible to making changes and experimenting with how you manage your time if you find that something isn't working. But once you find what works, stick to it and make sure you continue to frequently review and update your task list.

If you happen to be clueless when it comes to what time management techniques are available to you, find a website or purchase a book, DVD or online course to help you with your time management skills. Investing in a time management course is just that, an investment. The benefits of effective time management will repay you hundred-fold over the course of your life.

# Key #9: What You Think Doesn't Matter, What Your Professor Thinks Does

You will encounter many professors who will probably tell you that this Key is not true. They will tell you that any exam answer is potentially right if your rationale and logic are solid. To an extent, they are correct. But remember, professors are people too and can make mistakes. The classroom is your first courtroom and the professor is your first judge or jury. If you write a well-reasoned answer that adopts the view of the professor, he or she is less likely to see the flaws in the argument. That argument will sound inherently correct. It will make sense to the professor. They have defended many of these arguments against attacks from their peers (who are already lawyers, judges or law faculty) and they haven't changed their view yet. So what makes you think you'll be able to change their mind? Now, let me be extremely clear, there is NO substitution for a well-reasoned answer. **A well reasoned answer that adopts a contrary view would do better than one that adopts the professor's view but lacks the proper logical reasoning.**

During class, it's important to note the substance of what the professor is saying (the case law) as well as how the professor got there (the logical reasoning). Understanding how your professor reasons through a case can be very telling. Don't just pay attention to the answers. The questions or better yet, the line or sequence of questions is just as important, if not more important.  If you get into the habit of exploring cases and issues in the same manner as your professor, you are WAY AHEAD of your classmates.  When you review your class notes, try to figure out why your professor asked each particular question.  Why was it first, second, last, etc.?  Why did it follow the previous question and why was it before the following question?  The next time you finish reading a case, try to explore the case using a similar logic and sequence of questions.

What articles has your professor written?  Read them.  These articles are often a glimpse into the professor's real viewpoint.  In class, some cases may require your professor to advocate a viewpoint that is contrary to his or her actual viewpoint to insure that someone plays devil's advocate.

Visit the professor during office hours to discuss topics discussed in class.  This is especially true when you come upon a ruling or idea you disagree with.  You'll get a better understanding of why the professor takes a different viewpoint and you'll understand how to better articulate an opposing view.  The exam is not the time to express your personal views or opinions.  You can do that during class, after class with the professor or your peers, or after you become a law professor yourself.  During the exam, your goal is to get the best grade possible and the shortest route to that grade is by writing a well-reasoned answer that mimics the professors' train of thought and outcomes.

This last point may come off as pretty shallow advice and makes exams sound too subjective.  But it's actually very good training for your life as a lawyer. For most of your career, your work will be judged subjectively. The partners you work for will expect your logic to make sense to them. I am NOT saying that you should ever make up law or write something contrary to what your research presents just to please a partner. However, make sure you explore ALL the reasonable possibilities and provide the information in a way that makes it easy for the partner to process.

You will often work for several partners, just as you have several professors. So it is good practice to get into the habit of learning each professor just as you will have to learn each partner. Your clients will also judge your work subjectively. If all you ever do is bluntly give them bad news, you will not have many clients. Your juries will not necessarily think like you. Writing exams that cater to your professor is no different than using what you know about your jury to create persuasive arguments that they understand and accept. Again, your professor is your first jury. Make sure you put yourself in the best position to WIN your first case.

# Key #10: There Is NO Substitution For Doing The Work

Key #10 is rather unpleasant but extremely true. In life and law school, there are no short cuts. There are no magic bullets. The work you put in will reflect what result you get out. You may hear many older students tell you the contrary. It's not uncommon to get a low grade in a class where you worked extremely hard. It's equally possible to get good grades in classes you barely read for or attend. However, such instances are more exception than the rule. It's similar to the gambler who brags about winning $1000 but fails to mention that (s)he lost $5000 to "win" the $1000. The gambler actually is telling the truth. It's just that people tend to remember shocking situations and forget common situations. The more common situation is if you don't read for or attend a class, you will not do as well as you could have in that class. Being in class also helps to give your professor the impression that you are working hard in his or her class, which can lead to favorable job recommendations and better grades in his or her class.

You will realize during law school that there never seems to be enough time. Don't worry about this because you can't control it. But stay focused and motivated to do all the work, reading, etc. you need to do to be successful (including all of the great Keys listed here). When it feels like more than you can finish, press on and continue to do your best. Many times, I just needed one or two more hours to finish an outline or memorandum after I took extended breaks because I convinced myself that there was no way I could finish.

More importantly, I am a firm believer of the saying, "Work smarter, not harder." Putting in the work doesn't mean that you can't work smart. Realize that the word "work" is still right there in the saying. As you mature as a law student, you will get better and faster at doing the work. You will find ways to do the work more efficiently without sacrificing quality. However, you will never get to the point where you are faster and more efficient if you do not get in the habit of doing the work up front. These Keys are about becoming a successful law student and developing a foundation that you can later build upon to become a successful lawyer, judge, or law professor. As a legal professional there will always be work to do.

Like anything else in life, you learn by doing. It doesn't feel very good while you are going through it but it helps to shape you and make you better. It's no different from exercising or lifting weights. Unfortunately, your muscles aren't going to grow without a lot of hard work and some soreness. In the end, what doesn't kill you only makes you stronger.

# Key #11: Be An Active Listener

There will be many times in class when the professor has someone else in the hot seat and the only thing you are thinking is, "I'm glad that isn't me." Well, it's okay to think that... quickly... but then move on to more helpful thinking. Become an active listener. Being an active listener means that you are engaged in the conversation as if you are the one the professor is grilling. Try to answer every question the professor asks, silently to yourself, as if you are the one in the professor's line of fire.

Passive listening allows you to "think" you understand the material. Have you ever had someone explain something to you and think you understand everything, only to realize a little later, you don't remember a thing? That's passive listening. You feel like you are getting it because you are listening passively and jot down everything you think is important. However, when you listen actively, you realize how much you don't understand, especially when you continue to get the answers wrong.

If you continue to listen actively and answer questions to yourself, there isn't much difference when the professor calls on you. When the professor calls on you, you'll be used to coming up with the (hopefully) correct answers at the pace the professor expects. You'll be used to thinking through the question and providing answers.

People remember information better when they are listening actively. Instead of thinking back and trying to remember what your professor said the answer was to this or that… you'll remember that it was exactly what you answered or exactly opposite of what you answered, etc.

It also provides yet another reason to make sure that you are prepared for class. Often the most prepared lawyers are the most successful lawyers. This Key is a way to practice being prepared. Get in the habit now of being as prepared as you can for when you might be put on the spot unexpectedly.

# Key #12: Class Structure: General Rule, Narrow, Exception/Expansion

There are some things that no one ever cares to tell you because they don't realize it or don't think it's important enough to tell you. This is one "Key" that I didn't fully realize until well into law school. For me, knowing this just made all of my classes easier to follow and understand.

Realize how the cases in the book are organized. The reading is sometimes confusing because the cases that introduce the information don't seem to fit well with what you know about the world. When you realize that the first few cases just introduce the general rule or the concept of the rule, it helps digest the case as just an introduction. The initial cases are generally followed by later cases that help narrow or shape the rulings in the initial cases. Over time, circumstances arise that make it clear that a few loopholes in the initial cases need to be closed. Then, a few cases may appear that cut out an exception to the rule or expand a portion of the rule when the courts realize they went a little too far or over corrected.

Of course there are exceptions to this format, but it's generally the case during your first year of law school. Once I learned this, I could look at the table of contents and get a much better idea and understanding of the various sections we studied. At times, if I was confused with a ruling or disagreed with a ruling, I could look at the table of contents and begin to understand how that rule would evolve in later cases. Learning this information alone, helped to bring a lot of sanity to my law school life.

# Key #13: Start Writing NOW

Listen very carefully. **It always takes longer to write your memos and briefs than you can ever imagine during law school (and often during law practice as well).** So it's important to start right away. Start your research, start your outline, just be sure to start something. Just make sure you are getting something down on paper right away. You can always go back and clean it up.

There are several reasons to start early. One reason is that as you start to research, you sometimes find that your early assumptions are incorrect (sometimes exactly the opposite of reality). You need time to reassess how to write your paper when this happens.

After you develop your outline, you'll realize that you will sometimes need to make significant changes to the structure and flow of your paper just because of one or two cases you end up finding later in the research process.

I didn't really learn the proper writing process until I was in law school. For me, before law school, writing a paper often consisted of preparing an outline (if I even did that) and then cramming in as much accurate information as I could on the night or two before the paper was due. Sometimes I might add in a quick review to check for flow and spelling. That was a horrible way to write. However, many of us were able to get away with it in undergrad so we think we can continue with those same bad habits. If you think that will work in law school, you are WRONG.

What we were turning in to our professors in undergrad is a very shaky first draft in a law school. You will need to write several drafts before your paper is anywhere near done.

In order to edit your drafts properly, you also need to spend some time away from them. I don't mean to eat your dinner and come back. I mean take a day or two away from the paper. That way, it will be a little less like reading something you wrote yourself. It's important that you be your own devil's advocate as you review your paper. Is the logic clearly presented and easy to follow? Does the logic even make sense? Did you leave out information that the reader needs in order to understand the flow but that you neglected to include because YOU already knew the information. Remember, the reader didn't do any research so you have to take the reader step by step without taking any leaps in logic or leaving out any supporting information.

Lastly, including and editing your case cites is not fun. It can take forever. Actually, it does take forever or maybe time enters another dimension that just makes it feel like it's standing still. So, even if you are done with the substance of your paper, you still have to make sure that your cases are cited correctly, etc. You'll have to make sure you save PLENTY of time for that task until you've done it enough times that it becomes a piece of cake.

# Key #14: Skim, Read, Brief

This method will help you avoid having the Sixth Sense movie moment in reading cases. Ever read something, think it all makes sense and at the end, you realize how much you missed and how you were ultimately focused on all the wrong things? Then, when you read it again, you realize that the clues were there all along.

It's important to remember law cases are not novels. Like most normal people, you are probably used to reading things from beginning to end. And in law school, we often read from beginning to end while trying to retain as much information as possible. However, law cases are not novels. You don't have to wait until the end to find out the "answer" or the conclusion. Find out the answer right away. It will help you understand what's important.

This sequence will become immensely important early on in law school. During the beginning of your first year in law school, you are still getting used to reading cases, trying to figure out what is important, etc. The language of the cases can often be confusing and the concepts within the cases can be even more confusing. So, the first thing you should do is quickly skim the case. Just get a quick general idea of what the case is about and how the court ruled. Don't worry about retaining any information yet.

After skimming the case, read the case. You should read for understanding but don't get too bogged down if you run into a thing or two that seems a little confusing. You don't have to read for 100% understanding but make sure you are following any twist and turns in logic or case law. Once you are done reading the case, go back and brief the case. This time, you'll want as close to a complete understanding as possible. However, you've already skimmed the case and read it so it should be a little easier to pick out the information that is important.

At the end of the day, that's what you want. You want to be able to identify the pertinent (or "material") information within the case and be able to identify the IRAC (the Issue, the Rule, the Analysis and/or Application, and the Conclusion). That's much easier to do once you know how the case turns out. This process allows you locate all of the important information while avoiding a situation where something you initially thought was important ends up being considered as a minor detail and vice versa.

I know this sounds like it will take a lot of time. However, you will find it actually saves you time. Reading at a slow pace in order to comprehend the cases as soon as you encounter them will often eat up an enormous amount of time. So you will ultimately save time if you skim first, read for general understanding second, and then brief the case for a better understanding, to help you remember the information, and for ease of locating important information during class or exam study. And remember, your grade is all about the exam so having the cases briefed early will save you time when you start to create your outline. (*See Key #25 for more on creating outlines.*)

# Key #15: Look Up The Definitions And Use The Words

Sometimes, during your first year, law school will seem more like you are sitting in a foreign language class than a law class. It may seem obvious that you should look up the definitions to words that you don't know. Unfortunately, many law students simply don't. Instead you'll find students using context clues, etc. Don't be one of those students. Sometimes a true understanding of a decision may turn on the precise meaning of one word. I looked up more words in law school than at any other point in my life.

Also, you should have a good grasp of all the "terms" used in a particular class because it will help your exam performance. Professors are busy and I'm sure they hate grading exams as much or almost as much as law students hate taking them. Even if they don't hate grading exams, it's human nature to glaze over every once in a while when reading page after page of similar writings. What do you think happens when one exam isn't the same because it's missing some of the common terms that the professor is expecting? I'm hoping you answered that that paper gets extra scrutiny and a lower score. So the converse is sometimes also true. You'll have a chance to pick up a few points on exams just by using the right words (or at least you won't lose a few points for not using the terms the professor is looking for).

How do you remember all of the terms without going crazy or having a photographic memory?  Simple, use the words.  Use the words often.  If you learn a few new words that day, use them whenever you can.  Make a joke of it if you have to.  Some terms will be easier to laugh at like "piercing the corporate veil"... I still crack up when I think about all the situations we applied that to.  Tell someone that his or her outfit is unconscionable.  You'll be surprised how many times your friends will correct you and tell you that you are not using the word correctly or that you will correct your friend's usage.  You'll also end up getting into real conversations about various topics that are tangent to the words you use or the cases, etc.  Yes, you may feel a bit like a nerd using all of the "legal lingo" or the "terms of art" that you learn in class.  But you'll be expected to know the words on your exams, for the bar exam, and as a lawyer.  Why not make that chore a bit more fun.  You might even develop a few terms that you pray a judge never says during trial for fear that you will crack up thinking about former classmates.  And let's be serious, you are in law school which means by default, you are probably already a bit of a nerd.  So get over it nerd.

# Key #16: Review Your Notes Each Day And Ask For Clarification The Next Day

This is a CHORE. But it's essential to making your life easier later. Think delayed gratification. It's not uncommon to miss several important comments during class because you were busy taking notes on a previous statement or simply got distracted for a minute. It's okay to miss the information as long as you find out what you missed shortly after class. You must review your notes shortly after taking them while the information and class session are still fresh in your memory.

You are reviewing your notes for several different reasons. First, you want to fill in any gaps if you missed anything. If you notice gaps of information in your notes, ask your classmates what they have in their notes. If all your classmates missed it as well, ask the professor the next day. Depending on the professor, you can ask before class starts or maybe even during class. If neither is a good option, visit the professor during office hours.

Second, you are obviously reviewing the notes to better understand the material. Sometimes, in class, you are forced to just get down as much as you can. In those instances, you often aren't processing what you are writing or listening actively. (*See Key #11 for more on active listening.*) After class, you are able to review your notes and figure out if you understand what you wrote. Sometimes, you may even be trying to determine if what you wrote even makes any sense. When you come across something that you don't understand, ask your classmates. Once again, if they can't help, ask your professor the next day.

Thirdly, the new material you cover in class generally builds upon an understanding of earlier material (at least within each section of material). So if you don't understand the earlier material (as well as you possibly can at the time... because you may not completely grasp the material until near the end of the semester) you'll have greater difficulty with the later material. It's not uncommon to hear stories of students who never quite understood a topic during class but figured it out during exam study. All of a sudden, the whole class makes a lot more sense to them. You never know what one concept or issue will be the glue that binds it all together for you. So treat everything you learn in class like it could be the glue that brings it all together for you. Reviewing your notes regularly gives you an opportunity to have those "aha moments" earlier in the semester.

Finally, reviewing the information while it's still fresh will help solidify it in your memory making it easier to recall and remember when you are outlining and studying for exams.

# Key #17: Take Your Research And Writing Class Seriously

In some schools, this class is pass/fail. Don't use this as a reason to brush this class off. I get it. If you receive the same reward for just barely passing, why put in the extra effort? Plus, you're already pressed for time so one of your classes has to suffer. If that's your line of thought, make sure that this isn't the class that you decide not to take seriously.

You may or may not use what you learn in any of your other classes. As a lawyer, you WILL use what you learn in your research and writing class. It's the cornerstone of all we do. Before any case sees the light of a courtroom, a countless number of briefs, motions, and memorandums have been written. There is no other way to put this. Invest in your future. Not only will it help you later as a lawyer, it will help you in your near future as well. The IRAC style of writing is what will also be expected of you on your law school exams (or some other variation like CIRAC, IRAAC or CIRAAC, etc). For those unfamiliar with IRAC, it simply stands for Issue, Rule, Analysis and/or Application, and Conclusion. There is a good chance that you'll be using it for the rest of your law career. Get used to it, learn it, and learn to love it.

It's often easier for law students to put forward more effort, study harder and pay better attention in classes that focus on topics they are interested in as a possible career. And often, your assignments in your research and writing class will be on a topic of law that you are utterly uninterested in.  Fight the urge to slack off in this class.  Regardless of the area of law you ultimately focus on as a lawyer, you'll be using what you learned in research and writing everyday of your career.

What lots of students don't realize until it's almost too late is that your ability to quickly and accurately research a topic is extremely valuable to your future law firm.  While in law school, the legal research companies give you unlimited searching ability without time limits or costs... to get you hooked of course.  (I'm not comparing them to drug dealers but I am comparing the first-hit-is-free sales process to the one supposedly used by some drug dealers).  Well, after law school, you pay for access.  If not you, your law firm will generally pay by either the minute or by the search.  Searches can get very expensive very quickly if you aren't efficient.  So the better you are at researching quickly without sacrificing accuracy, the more valuable you become to the firm you are working for whether it be a large firm, small firm or your own firm.

# Key #18: Learn To Tab, Save Your Work, and Save Your Work Again

**This Key sounds silly but it's so true and SO important.** If you have the luxury of an open book exam during law school, you'll realize the necessity of good tabbing. During the crunch of an exam, you don't have time to look through your whole outline for each new question to find the relevant section of your outline. Having a good and easy to navigate tabbing system can be your best friend.

The best outline is NO help if you can't find what you are looking for in a timely fashion. There are always students who are extremely proud of their outlines who eventually don't do so well on exams because while the outline was accurate and beautiful, the student couldn't find the information when they needed it. By following the Keys in *33 Keys To Law School Success*, you'll be prepared to ace the exam without an outline. Still, it's always comforting to know you can do a quick double check to make sure you got the case name correct, etc. Tabbing may seem like an afterthought but it's potentially a big part of your law school exam success.

Like clockwork, every year, during exam study period, several students face the unfortunate situation of losing all of their work. The culprit can be a computer virus, a dropped laptop, a stolen laptop, a confused click of the wrong button or even a flood in your apartment. Whatever, the reason, the result is the same. You have now lost hours and hours of your hard work. Don't press your luck. Get renters insurance and know it can happen to you. Be prepared.

In order to help protect yourself from facing this particular disaster, **you should save your work in various locations**. Of course it's on your computer but make sure it's on a jump drive or external drive. Maybe even two jump drives. You might decide to keep one in your apartment and one in your car. Make it a part of your regular routine to save your work. It would work perfectly to do your saving after you've just completed your regular periodic outlining or briefing. (*See Key #14 for more on briefing your cases.*) You might also look into storing the documents in a hosted site or in a cloud that you can access from anywhere. I don't suggest paying for a service but at least you know your work is safe.

Print out hard copies as well. Without a doubt technology can find a way to go completely crazy on you just when you need it the most. With two electronic backups and one or two paper backups, you should be in a much better situation if you so happen to fall victim of an ill-timed digital catastrophe.

# Key #19: Apply For Jobs On Day One

This may be one of the most valuable law school Keys I was told. Many 1L's (first year law students) don't initially realize that there are rules governing how soon companies can recruit or even contact 1L's for employment. Actually, they are supposed to turn you away if you stumble upon a reception, meeting, recruiting dinner, etc. before the appropriate time. Employers are supposed to inform you that they cannot talk to you even if you contact them.

Currently, you cannot utilize your career services resources until November 1st of your first year and employers are not allowed to have contact with you until December 1st of your first year. While that will seem light years away at the beginning of the semester, get prepared now. While you cannot contact potential employers, you can get ready for November and December 1st. Work on your resume and cover letter well in advance. Have other classmates review them for you. Get samples from the various student organizations you have joined. (*See Key #30 for more on student organizations.*) Check out books from the library or buy books from the bookstore. Just make sure that your resume and cover letter are done BEFORE November 1st.

November and December will be a hectic time of year as a 1L so you don't want to have extra work to do. When November 1st rolls around, get your hands on the NALP (National Association for Law Placement) firm directory. The directory will provide contact information and stats on firms by geography, practice area, etc. Begin your research. Create a database with all the contact information for the firms you are interested in applying to. Cast your net widely. If there is any possibility that you would be interested in working for that firm during your first summer, include them. You can always turn down a job offer if you decide it's not the right firm for you. You can't go back and add a firm and have the same effect if you don't get any offers. It will be too late.

Create a merge file with your cover letter, merge the database and letter and make sure you have your letters ready to put in the mail on December 1st. Put your letters in the mail ON December 1st. You can't do it before, and you don't want to do it any later. As a side note: it's helpful to create a full name and an appropriate acceptable shortened name for each law firm. Use the full name for the address field and use the shortened name within the letter. It makes it look a little less like a form letter. Be sure to review each and every letter and edit them appropriately after you have merged them. There are often small spacing glitches and errors that will ruin your first impression if you don't correct them.

Why do you want to send your letters out on December 1st? Some reasons are obvious but others aren't as obvious until the spring semester. First, it's typically better to be early rather than late. Lots of law firms hire in a manner that is similar to what law schools call rolling admissions. That means it's easier to get hired early on when they have more spaces available. As the available spaces dwindle, firms become pickier and pickier about whom they are hiring.

Secondly, you'll be able to schedule your firm interviews during your break between semesters. You'll be more available to travel if necessary and you don't have to worry about missing classes, etc. Law firms also slow down a little bit at the end of the year so they'll have a little more time to schedule interviews as well.

Thirdly, if you interview during your break, your interview skills will sometimes matter more than your grades. Law schools are notorious for getting grades back to you very late. You may not get your first semester grades until well into February or March. If you follow the plan in this Key, you'll have the opportunity to receive a job offer before or right after returning to school for your second semester. Therefore, during your interviews you can honestly answer that you don't yet have your grades but you think you did very well on your exams. That's a lot easier than trying to explain away a single or a couple of bad grades. Often, as long as you don't completely bomb on your exams, you'll be able to keep your offer. If not, you'll still have the opportunity to apply and interview for law firm summer jobs with the rest of the 1L's.

1L recruiting season isn't until the middle of the second semester. You'll be busy in the swing of classes again and your grades will be out. Plus, you'll be competing with the entire 1L class at your school as well as across the country for interviews, let alone jobs. Get your job BEFORE all that chaos ensues.

# Key #20: Don't Always Believe Your Classmates

Unfortunately, most if not all, law schools are full of Type A personalities. When you add the fact that most law school classes are graded on a curve (which means if you get an A someone else will have to get a grade equal distance below the curve to balance it all out, and vice versa) you have the perfect formula for real life reality show hijinx. Alliances, sabotaging, lying, etc. are rampant at many law schools. (**Refresh yourself on Key #1 and be sure to research your potential schools to find out which schools may be worse than others.**)

You can expect all types of mind games from your peers. Everything from saying that they never study or just "skimmed" the assigned reading to telling you they aced the exam. Some common lies are: I didn't understand anything I read last night; No I haven't even started that yet (researching, writing, studying, etc.); I finished that in x minutes (some time period that is unrealistically short); I'm not even going to study for that exam; I never read for that class; I aced that exam; I completely understood what the professor was talking about, etc.

Reality shows have alliances. The law school versions of alliances are study groups. You'll find that some study groups form that you aren't allowed into or didn't know about. People you thought were your friends will choose someone else in hopes of creating a better chance at "survival." There is nothing wrong with them wanting to create a study group that insures their success.  Just realize that if they don't think you are an asset to the study group, you will usually be excluded from those groups.  **The funny thing is you don't have to worry.**  Many of the decisions regarding study groups end up being based on the wrong factors because they are formed too early.  Discuss your cases with any and everyone freely.  Get input from everyone.  But wait to form a true study group until closer to the end of the semester.  If you follow the Keys in *33 Keys To Law School Success*, you'll have your pick of study partners.

Keep in mind sabotage too is a part of the reality show.  You don't have to be in law school long before you start to hear about (or experience) other students hiding resource books or ripping out pages to make it more difficult for you to find and use those resources.  I was fortunate that I chose one of the coolest law schools on the planet, UVA Law School (another shameless but sincere plug).  We rarely had problems with sabotage, etc.  However, my close friends at other law schools had stories you wouldn't believe and they had lots of them.

It all boils down to one rule.  **Know thyself**.  Regardless of what another student tells you, you have to do what YOU have to do.  If it takes you an hour to study what they said should only take 15 minutes, take the hour to study.  If you feel it really should have taken less time, work on creating more efficient study habits... but also remember that, unlike some of your peers, you are simultaneously preparing for the end of the semester so it may take you a little longer here and there.

Once the exam is over, forget about it.  Obsessing over it AFTER you have taken it will not change your grade.  Listening to your frenemies (enemies posing as friends) discuss all the possible answers you didn't include does NOTHING at this point.  Focus on your next exam and remain confident, positive and prepared.  Don't let your peers throw you off your game.  At least half of successful exam taking is having the proper mental attitude throughout preparation and during the exam.

This Key makes it that much more important to develop REAL friendships during law school with good people who happen to have good study habits as well.  (**For more on this see Key #21.**)  Find people you can rely on who can also rely on you.

# Key #21: Share Your Work With Friends

This is an incredibly controversial Key for a law school student. Many see law school as an all out competition. And law schools definitely encourage that view. If the curve is set to a grade of a B, then if I get an A, someone else will get a C to balance out my A. And if someone else gets an A, there is more of a chance that I'll get a C. But given the jaded nature of the previous Key, you'll need some good karma to balance out the negativity.

Fight off the pressure to become a worse person. And if you are already a horrible person, (first of all you suck but) make this the time in your life that you work on becoming a better person. Whether you believe in karma, God, the universe or something else, you can probably find many reasons why it's better to share than not to share. First, let me clear something up. I said to share your work with FRIENDS. So I'm not saying that you should share your hard work with any and everyone who asks you for it. But we're talking about a friend. We're not talking about someone who has ignored you until he or she needs something (there's even an argument for sharing with that person as well but this isn't the proper space to have that discussion). Your friend isn't just mooching off of you for your outline. Your friend will be around and you'll need plenty from your friend at some point in law school or life. Maybe it will not come in the form of an outline, but things have a way of balancing out over time. At the end of the day, what goes around comes around and you never know when you'll unexpectedly need help from someone. Life happens. Why not be the type of person that your peers are more than willing to help if they see you need it?

Just in case altruism isn't a good enough reason for you, there are also other reasons to share your work with your friends. Your friends will sometimes find errors in your outline and bring them to your attention. There is nothing worse than studying the wrong information for the entire semester only to find out during an exam cram session that you had it wrong the whole time. It's better to find out sooner than later (if you follow my Keys you'll find out a lot sooner than exam time). You wouldn't be the first person to completely reverse the meaning of a sentence by forgetting the word "not" in the sentence.

If you ever borrow someone else's outline you'll quickly come to a shocking revelation. You don't completely understand many parts of the outline. You see, an outline is a condensed version of your briefs (which are already a shortened version of the cases). (*More on Outlines in Key #25.*) Often, in order to shorten the outline, you will develop your own personal style of shorthand. You'll include words or phrases that jog your memory and represent entire paragraphs or pages of information. But those phrases are keyed to your mind and how your mind works, your personal experiences and expressions. So honestly, even if you share your outline with someone, it should be MUCH more helpful to you than it will ever be to him or her. They will still have to do considerable work to your outline to make sure that they understand all the rules and concepts that you have condensed down to simple phrases or sentences. And don't forget that it works both ways. If you get an outline from someone, you still have to do considerable work on it to personalize it to your mind and memory.

Finally, don't forget to check your schools honor code or policy. As with any of the Keys in this book, you should NOT do any of them if they contradict your school's rules or policies. This book is about helping you succeed in law school. Getting into trouble with your school would be the quite the opposite of success. Can you say #epicfail?

# Key #22: Get To Know Students In Other Graduate Schools On Your Campus

Law school can quickly become all encompassing and a pretty suffocating place. (In a good all encompassing and suffocating way.) It helps to get out and break the routine. It is especially helpful if you meet other graduate students on campus. You may be surprised to hear that they too are wondering why they signed up for the punishment of two, three, four or more additional years of school. Let's face it, sometimes, misery loves company. But breaking away from your law school friends and hang out with someone who doesn't act like they fell out of the law student cookie cutter mold will be helpful to your sanity. It's also good to hang around people that you aren't competing with for grades and who could care less if you know what you are talking about while you are being cold called by Socrates incarnate.

Friendships grow exponentially, not linearly. What do I mean? Well, when you make friends with one med school student, you tend to meet several of his or her classmates. They often have a few friends in other grad schools you'll meet and the cycle continues. You'll be surprised how quickly you'll know a sizeable portion of the very small grad school community on your campus. Spending a few evenings listening to schoolmates' debate issues they are discussing in their classes can be just what you need to break the monotony of legalese. An even better evening would be one in which none of you discuss anything related to school. As an added benefit, you'll sometimes pick up some information that will help you develop a better well-rounded view of topics, that have nothing to do with law.

More than just being a breath of fresh air and a break from law school jargon, other graduate students on your campus often become a strong, deep, influential and profitable network of friends. I'm not suggesting that you go into any friendship with ulterior motives. However, isn't it a great thing if friends you make during law school become a great source of referral business later in life? Just like you, your friends will have a wide web of friends in various areas of expertise. Eventually everyone needs an attorney or knows someone looking for a referral to an attorney. Your friends will think of their lawyer friend... **you**. And you most likely will reciprocate the favor. You'll think of your friends when someone you meet asks you for a referral to a doctor, educator, therapist, etc.

# Key #23: It's Not About How You Sound In Class, It's About The Exam

You may eventually have a class or two where class participation is a part of your grade. In those classes, this Key does not apply. However, your grade in the great majority of your classes will be determined by a single final exam. Yes, you heard me correctly, one final exam. So why in the world are you so stressed by your bad performance in class? Of course, it's better to knock it out of the park in class as well as on the exam. However, if you happen to get called on in class and suddenly realize that you have no clue what the case is about, or what the class is about for that matter... don't sweat it. Chalk it up as a learning experience and make sure you continue to do all of the other things you should be doing (i.e.: the other Keys).

There may be times where you remain clueless until a week, a day, maybe even the night before the exam (although these Keys should help minimize being clueless for that long). Trust that you will eventually get there and keep working toward the goal. Think the tortoise and the hare. Be the tortoise. If you realize that you are far more clueless than your peers and study partners in a particular class, ask for help and put in a little extra time studying for that class. The person you ask for help can be anyone from a peer advisor to a professor to the Dean of Students. Just make sure that it's someone who will point you in the right direction and assist with getting you the help you need to do well in that particular class.

If you want to repair your image with the professor, start to visit him or her during office hours (*See Key #3 for more on getting to know your professors.*) Get better prepared for his or her class and volunteer to answer when another student is stumped. BEWARE: Some professors frown on "saving" a classmate so play it by ear. Also be prepared to answer more than that one question if you volunteer. Assume that you have volunteered as a complete substitute for the hot seat. You didn't die the first time you couldn't answer a question and you won't this time either.

You'll come across students who sound great in class but have trouble putting it all together on an exam. You want to do well on the exam. Period. Not impress your friends in class. So everything you do with respect to studying should be focused on doing well on the exam. That's why you brief cases, outline, etc. during the semester. You want to make exam study easier. Of course, you hope to do well in class and on the exam but inevitably, you'll get called on the one solitary day that you are not prepared. Just remember, your grade is ALL about the exam.

# Key #24: Study Using Old Exams

This may not always be possible but it is a MUST when it is possible. The first thing you MUST do is find out your school's policy on usage of old exams. DO NOT do anything that is prohibited by your law school. If your law school allows the use of old or sample exams, find as many as you can. Where are sample exams? At some law schools, the law library will store old sample exams. Student organizations may also have sample exams. Other students who have already taken the professors class may have an old exam.

Find and copy the sample exams right at the beginning of the semester. Why? Because some professors will swap out sample exams stored in the library during the first few weeks of classes. If you get there before your professor swaps them out, you'll get two sets of sample exams for that class. I actually suggest checking for sample exams at least three times. At the very beginning of the semester, in the middle of the semester and shortly before exam period begins. But remember, if you are unsure if using sample exams is allowed, ask the professor or a reliable administrator BEFORE you do any of the above.

Studying from old exams can give you an idea of the way the professor may choose to structure the exam. Does the professor use long fact patterns, short questions, definition questions, or even multiple-choice questions? The sample exams give you a glimpse at the types of questions the professor may ask and the level of preparation that may be required. Do the exam questions reference a case? That would mean that you should be familiar with the names of the cases. Do the questions reference a particular judge or justice's opinion? If so, you'll want to make sure you include a few notes regarding any significant class discussions about a particular judge's opinion. ALWAYS assume that the actual exam will be more difficult than the sample exam. Don't get tricked into relaxing because the sample exam is "easy" to you. Again, ALWAYS assume that the actual exam will be more difficult than the sample exam.

Can't find any old exams or aren't allowed to use old ones? Make up questions and hypotheticals with your study partners. There were a few times when a couple of our study group hypotheticals were extremely close to exam questions. You can imagine our excitement when we read the question and knew that we had thoroughly discussed this question a few nights before the exam. Make the hypotheticals difficult. Do your best to channel the spirit of your professor for the particular class when designing and wording your hypothetical. Make sure to include any subject matter that was particularly confusing during the semester. The exam study period is the time to figure out those complex issues, not run from them.

Don't simulate exam conditions right away. Initially, give yourself as much time as necessary to answer the questions. Once you have answered the question, review your study materials and improve your answer based on what you find. Then, review your answer with your study partners. Walk through the questions and the possible answers with your study mates. Look up information in your outlines and books again to make sure that you have covered all the potential issues. Complete the question by helping each other walk through the thought process and the general outline of how to address the question. During your next study session, start by answering the same questions you previously discussed, but under time constraints. Review your answer with your study mates to quickly address the missed issues or information before moving on to new questions.

As you get more comfortable with the information, you can start to take portions of the sample exams. First give yourself a little extra time. Gradually decrease your time limits until you eventually stay confined to exam conditions. Once you have answered a sample exam question under time constraints, take the sample question and your answer to your study mate or someone you trust and ask him or her to critique it for you. When looking for someone to review your exam answers, ask around and find out who has previously gotten an A or other high grade in the class and ask that person to critique your practice answer (but remember its exam period for them as well so be considerate of their time and understanding if they don't have time to help). In some instances you can take the sample question and answer directly to your professors and ask them how they would improve the sample answer.

# Key #25: Make Outlines For Exams

Outlines are often simply a shortened version of your case briefs (which themselves are shorten versions of the cases) with a few extra notes and phrases that communicate a wealth of information. This is not always the case but most law texts are organized by topic. Therefore, a group of cases covering the same issue are generally already grouped together for you. You'll find a few exceptions but hopefully it will be clear to you when the exception occurs.

An excellent way to start your outline is to look at the table of contents in the text. That can often become the skeleton version of your outline. Of course, you'll want to alter the order of the contents of the outline based on the order your professor teaches the course. The syllabus can be an excellent indication of the changes you'll have to make to your outline. Since you've followed my Keys and you've been briefing your cases each day, making an outline is much less of an arduous task. (**See Key #14 for more on briefing cases.**) As a matter of fact, if you follow my Keys, your outline will be close to complete before your peers even get started on their outlines.

Periodically, you should review your case briefs and shorten them to create a preliminary outline for that section of cases. It makes sense to create the preliminary outlines after each topic or section in the table of contents is completely covered in class.

That way you have completed the concept and should have a general understanding of what you were supposed to learn from that group of cases. However, because of your schedule, it might make more sense for some of you to do it once a week. Do whatever works best for you. What's important is that you are creating your preliminary outline regularly, in bite size increments instead of waiting for the end of the semester. Also, before you create your outline for the current section, quickly review the portions of the outline that you have already created. This quick review will help reinforce the concepts, cases and terminology you have already learned and adds repetition over a longer period of time. The repetition will aid your ability to recall the information during your exams. Additionally, a quick review of completed sections of your preliminary outline may give further insight into previous or future topics.

Not only will doing it this way make life much easier for you at the end of the semester, it will also help you struggle through the concepts and better learn the material. Don't worry if you don't always COMPLETELY grasp the concepts. Trust that it will eventually come together. What's important is that you understand it better than you did before you started the outline. Most classes build from foundational material to more complex topics. Therefore, it's to your advantage to better understand the earlier material as it will help you understand the later material.

While other students are creating their outlines and reviewing their information for the first time, you should be able to review your outline and create an even more condensed version of your outline without sacrificing understanding or accuracy. And since you'll have a little more time than your peers, you'll have time to tab your outlines during exam period. Tabbing your outlines will make the information that much easier to find during the chaos of an exam. (*See Key #18 for more on tabbing your outline.*) You'll also be able to study from your outlines instead of having to carry around your big heavy backbreaking books at the end of the semester.

Yes you will be giving up a few hours during the semester that you wish you weren't giving up. But believe me when I say that you will be incredibly happy that you did it come exam time. There are few instances in education that are more stressful than law school exam period. Your preparation will save you a great deal of stress and put you on the path of acing your exams.

# Key #26: Simulate Exam Conditions When You Study

What I don't mean by this Key is to start off studying by taking timed practice tests over and over. You should take timed practice exams, but that shouldn't come until later in your preparations when you have a better understanding of the material. However, if you know that your exam will be in the morning, try to study for that class in the morning. Get your brain used to thinking about that material at that particular time of day. If you know where you will be taking the exam, if possible, try to study in that location. Get your brain used to thinking about the material in that room. The more you do to simulate exam conditions, the more your brain will kick into a subliminal cruise control. It's like subconsciously jogging memory. The way our minds work is such a mystery. There are so many things that we still don't know about how our minds work. However, over time I have come to realize that stimuli such as time of day, familiarity of environment, smell, etc. can influence the recall of information.

As you get more comfortable with the study materials, you should begin to practice small sections of the exam. For instance, try answering one question under a time constraint similar to what you expect on the exam. After answering that question, review your answer. Go through your outline to see if you forgot anything. Did you miss any issues?  How did your study partners answer the question?  Have your study partners review your answer and tell you what they think you could have done better. Figure out the best answer for the question with your study partners.  If you can't agree, you know you have something to ask your professor or other classmates.

Try the question again during the next study session.  You'll be amazed that sometimes, you actually forget some of the information.  Figure out what you forgot or answered incorrectly this time around. Hopefully, you are getting closer to a perfect score on that question.  Also, it shouldn't take as long to re-answer the question the second, third, etc., times.  Repeat the process every study session until you get the question close to 100% correct.  Don't spend any significant time discussing the answers as you should have exhausted the discussion the first time you answered it.  At this point it's just a matter of memorization.

Chances are you won't have that question on the exam.  However, some of the same issues may be in a different question.  You have built up a memory bank of various other issues that may also arise in conjunction with that issue.  Be sure to look for any of those commonly tangent issues if you spot one on an actual exam question.

Take the sample question and your answer to your study partner or someone you trust and ask him or her to critique it for you.  Ask around and find out who previously got an A or other high grade in the class and ask that person to critique your practice answer. Be sure to be considerate of his or her time as everyone is preparing for exams. Don't get too upset if he or she does not have time to review your sample answer, it is exam period. Move on to someone else or just trust your study partner.

Once you start to feel like you have a decent grip on the study materials for that particular class, if time permits, try your best to simulate the exam. Use only the materials you will be allowed to use on the exam. Try to spend approximately the same amount of time as the length of the exam on your "trial run" of the exam. Sometimes, practicing the marathon of sitting still and concentrating on that subject matter over an extended period of time is just as crucial to your exam success as actually knowing the material. Exam fatigue is a real thing. Practice conquering it and figure out what helps you make it through the exam. Is it a good stretch half way through the exam period? Is it a cup of coffee or a bottle of water? A small snack or energy bar? You should experiment to find out what will help you maintain peak performance during your actual exam session. And remember that what you need for peak performance during the morning may be completely different than what you need during the evening.

Additionally, if possible, study using an old exam. This may not always be possible but it is a must when it is possible. *See Key #24 ("Study Using Old Exams") for more information regarding using old or sample exams to prepare for your actual exam.*

# Key #27: Use Your Resources

Before we begin this section, an important caveat: Every school has different rules and regulations so make sure you check to insure that you aren't breaking any school rules by following the advice below.

If this isn't the first year your professor has taught this particular course, ask any and everyone if he or she has notes or outlines from a previous year. A few things may change if there are recent developments but a bulk of the information will be the same. Also, make sure you ask for BOTH notes and outlines. Don't just ask upper-class students; be sure to ask any of your friends in the class as well. You never know when one of your classmates may have snagged a copy of an outline that he or she is willing to share with you.

Some schools even log old exams in the library. It doesn't hurt to make a copy of an old exam at the beginning of the semester and tuck it away until you need it later on. You never know if the professor will decide during the semester to change the copy of the old exam on file or remove it altogether. Some schools may even allow students to keep old copies of exams. If your school happens to be one of these schools, make sure you add exams to your request for notes and outlines.

There are often also commercially produced premade outlines and study guides that are keyed to your exact book. If it's in your budget, buy a copy. You may also find that someone has an old copy that he or she doesn't mind letting you borrow for the semester. These outlines can be extremely helpful, especially early in your first year.

Now that you have all these materials, what in the world do you do with them? These materials and study aides aren't very good if you don't know how to use them. The commercial outlines are best used as a reference AFTER you have created your own case briefs. Don't consult them until after you've read and briefed your cases. You'll be able to compare your briefs with the commercial outline to see if you are pulling the most relevant information from the cases. Did you get the correct ruling? Did you confuse dicta with relevant facts? Eventually, you'll get to the point where you won't have to consult the commercial outlines because your outlines and case briefs will be spot on. Truth be told, every once in a blue moon, you'll end up using the commercial outlines as a crutch. Don't get in the habit of it but when you are in a crunch for time, it's better to have reviewed the commercial outline before class than to have no clue what the cases are about.

Students generally created the old outlines you get from them at the end of the semester. Therefore, they sometimes provide a little better perspective of where you are headed and what this particular case means in the overall big picture. If done well, they will also include some interesting slants and perspectives offered by your professor that you don't necessarily get from commercial outlines or from reading the case on your own. Remember that any resources that are student made are liable to be extremely flawed. So again, make sure that these aids are adding to your exam preparation and do not become the bulk of or the full extent of your preparation.

I won't say a lot about old tests, as they are just a sample of what the professor decided to test the students on in an earlier semester. In some classes, it's a game of chance. There may be some consistency from year to year but not enough to bank on it. Generally, use the old test as practice exam questions near the end of the semester as you prepare for your exam. Discuss your answers with your study group to get different perspectives and to see what you may have missed. (**See Key # 24 for more on using old exams.**)

Old notes for that particular professor and subject are great. Many professors present the material like a prepared actor or comedian. They know exactly what they are going to say, including the so called off the cuff jokes here and there. So having old notes are like reading the book before seeing the movie. You'll know most of what's going to happen before you even set foot in class. Read and brief your cases, then read over the notes for the next day (again AFTER you have already prepared for class). You'll get a great glimpse into what your professor thinks is important and what's not.

Commercial study guides are often helpful when you are just lost and confused. They can offer a better summary of the concepts you should have pulled from the case that has you so confused. They also often offer a bit of context to help put the case in perspective with respect to the course in general. Unfortunately, commercial study guides can be a bit pricey and although they provide a good general overview of the material you are covering, they often don't provide much specific insight. They work great in the few instances when you've already reviewed the rest of the material but still don't have a clue what is going on.

# SECTION 3

# Setting Yourself Up
# For Success

# Key #28: Learn Westlaw AND Lexis AND Whatever New Comes Along In The Future

If you watch enough movies with gangsters or drug dealers, sooner or later you hear the theory of giving your product away for free (the first time) so that people get hooked and come back for more (and are willing to pay whatever price you want). Well I'm not calling the legal search engine providers drug dealers, but I'm definitely saying that their process for developing clients' sounds very familiar to what I've seen in a movie or two. But there are several reasons not to get "hooked" on just one of the search providers.

You have no way of knowing which of the providers your future employer will be using. If you only learn one, you will be faced with a steep learning curve after you are at your new firm. In other words, you'll take longer to get that important last minute memo done. Or more importantly, you may not have found all the relevant case law or know how to completely locate contradictory law or past rulings that alter the impact of what you may have found.

Even if the law firm you end up working at has access to both providers, they may be priced differently. YES, it costs law firms to use these legal research services. I know that you get free access while you are in law school and you can search to your heart's content, but after law school, it will cost you (or your firm) a pretty penny. Some firms pay by search, while some search based on time. If you are fluent on both search services you'll be able to use the provider that will result in the lowest charge to the firm. Trust me, it matters. The bottom line ALWAYS matters.

It's even worse if you decide to hang out your own shingle in the future. If you only know one research platform, you will be forced to pay whatever they charge to utilize a necessary research tool. Why back yourself into that corner if you don't have to?

Take the time to really learn how to most effectively and efficiently utilize the various research services while you are in school and it's free. There will be times when you MUST be absolutely sure that you have found everything that can be found on a matter. There will be other times when issues will arise at the last minute that must be included in a memo or brief. It's best if you are prepared.

# Key #29: Get Involved In The Community

There are many reasons why you should get involved in the local community. First of all, it's just the right thing to do. Whether or not you know it, the fact that you attend law school makes you more privileged than many of those in your community. There are many people in the area immediately surrounding your law school who are not nearly as fortunate as you. You are living in and drawing from their community, so give back to it as well. Secondly, doing good deeds creates positive karma, and who doesn't need good karma. Trust me, when exam period gets going, you'll want as much positive karma stored up as possible.

Getting involved in your surrounding community isn't just about giving. You'll be getting as well. I know it sounds cliché and corny but hey, sometimes the truth is corny. While in law school, it's easy to forget that you are a part of a larger world. Isolation leads to delusion. It's easy to forget that there are a lot of issues that people are dealing with everyday. I often found that I looked forward to those days that I was volunteering. There was nothing more refreshing than the ability to socialize and get to know a few non-lawyers. Talking to "regular" people who often (rightly or wrongly) look up to you as a law student and future lawyer has a way of keeping things in perspective. If you pay attention, you will learn a lot of lessons about life, love, the value of our possessions, etc. from these exceptional "regular" people. To be honest, I'm not sure why anyone would think that their profession makes them an expert on all things. Why wouldn't you learn something from others in the community?

What does getting involved in the community mean? It means whatever you want it to mean. Volunteer with a Big Brother Little Brother program, Habitat for Humanity, or some other program that focuses on helping those who are not currently as fortunate as you. Join a local bowling team, hiking club, skiing or jogging group, a social organization, etc. Do whatever allows you to get away from law school on a periodic basis and feel good about what you are doing at the same time. Make a difference and leave your surrounding community a better place when you graduate.

# Key #30: Get Involved
# With Organizations

Getting involved with various law school organizations has a wealth of benefits. Many of you are aware that organizations can help make you a well-rounded undergraduate student, which is good for your personal development as well as law school applications. Organizations can do the same for you in law school. And why do you want to be a well-rounded law school student? Other than it just being a good thing to continue your personal development, some law firms will actually prefer students who were involved in various organizations.

In addition to making you a more well rounded student and attractive job candidate, the people you get to know through organizations will often develop into lifelong friendships that mature beyond law school as well as potential business partners or sources of referral business. You'll meet people and expand your sphere of influence beyond what you would have without the organization. Law school organizations can give you additional support and a sense of community that may elude you if you only focus on reading cases and only meet students in your classes for three years.

Organizations are also a great place to begin or continue sharpening your skills as a leader. Take a leadership position in an organization or two. You will quickly learn your strong and weak points with respect to working with people, leading and managing others, building consensus, your ability to follow direction from others, training others, etc. At some point in your law career, you'll want to start taking on more of a leadership role, whether it be within a law firm or in a professional organization. You will be all the more effective if you've had a chance to work on your leadership skills during law school.

Additionally, leaders of organizations are presented with opportunities that are not presented to other law students. You may have the opportunity to meet with the Dean of your law school to help shape policies or provide crucial student input. You may be invited to fundraising functions in which you'll be mixing and mingling with the law school's biggest supporters and law firm recruiters. As the leader of an organization, you'll have the opportunity to leave a legacy by introducing or creating new programs and functions that continue on long after you have graduated. I truly believe that it's important to leave your law school community better than it was when you entered.

A hidden benefit of joining an organization is that they often have a wealth of resources that only members are privy to. Many organizations have old outlines, exams, textbooks, and notes that have been donated by graduating students who want to give back to an organization that they were a part of. It never hurts to have more quality study materials to help you prepare for exams as well as potentially save a couple dollars.

You shouldn't have a problem finding an organization or two that interests you. Law schools tend to have an organization for just about anything you can think of. There are organizations for various religious beliefs, cultures, sexual orientations, advocacy interests, hobbies, sports, etc. We even had organizations for the spouses of law students. If an organization that interests you doesn't exist, start it because inevitably, there will be others who have the same exact interests. I witnessed the start of at least 3 or 4 organizations during my time in law school. As a matter of fact, most of them sounded like pretty cool and interesting organizations.

# Key #31: Enroll In A Clinical Class

A clinical class or "clinic" is a class in which you typically get to work on real issues with practicing attorneys. A criminal defense clinic may consist of representing local indigent clients in misdemeanor cases. Yes, actually representing the clients in court (of course with the proper supervision of a practicing attorney). It is an opportunity to put all the theory into practice and it can often help bring the theory alive.

Clinics are great reminders of why you went to law school in the first place. No one goes to law school to sit in class and listen to professors. You go because you want to be a lawyer. Maybe you want to free the wrongfully accused. Maybe you want to help inventors protect their intellectual property. Maybe you want to bring justice to victims. Maybe you want to help aspiring artists negotiate fair contracts that protect their rights. Whatever your reason you'll probably be able to find a clinic to help you do just that while still in law school. (*See Key #1 for more on choosing the right school.*)

I continue to believe that the profession of law is a noble profession. I further believe we need more attorneys that are dedicated to helping others by providing quality, honest and ethical representation. Clinics help you begin to develop those skills earlier than your peers who don't participate in clinical classes.

As an added benefit, all other things being equal, employers prefer a new grad that has clinical experience over one who does not. Employers like the fact that your learning curve should be a little faster than the typical new law school graduate. Additionally, if you took a clinic and are still interested in that particular area of law, employers know that you are less likely to realize a year in (after they've spent all that time training you while paying you a salary) that you don't actually like that practice area.

On the other hand, you might find that you actually don't like the reality of practicing in an area of law that you thought you would like. It's much better to find out during school than after graduation. Finding out during school will allow you to explore other areas of law and/or other career paths that will utilize your law degree prior to accepting a job you might not like.

# Key #32: Realize That Later On, No One Will Care

During law school, at the end of each semester, it can feel like your life is hanging in the balance. You think to yourself, if you don't do well on this exam, you'll be considered a failure. Then to top off all that anxiety, after law school you are faced with taking the Bar Exam. Once again, your life hangs in the balance as you convince yourself that you MUST pass the bar on your first attempt.

Now I'm not going to tell you that your exams don't matter or that passing the bar is no big deal, because that just wouldn't be true. However, you should know that after practicing law for a few years, not many people will really care. What will matter more than your law school grades or when you passed the bar is whether or not you can produce a quality legal product and provide great customer service (your customer can be anything from a partner at your firm to a client of your very own firm).

So it's important to keep the big picture in mind and RELAX. Just make it onto the playing field. Yes, you should strive to do exceptionally well on all of your exams as well as the Bar Exam. However, it's not the end of the world if you slip here or there. Also, students tend to do a bit better on exams when they aren't paralyzed with fear. I'm not talking the healthy make you study harder fear. I'm talking the freeze up on the exam at the sight of any obstacle type of fear.

One caveat, your grades do matter when it comes to large firm recruiters. *(See Key #19 for advice on possibly reducing the impact of this fact.)* And some large firms will give you one or two chances to pass the bar while working for them before they ever so politely ask you to study without the distraction of working at their firm. So again, I'm definitely not saying that grades and bar passage aren't very important. However, there are rumors of Supreme Court Justices not passing the Bar Exam on their first attempt. If a Justice on the highest court in the land can take more than one attempt, well, why should any of us have any apprehension about having to take the exam more than once? There was a saying at our law school (which was possibly a saying at all law schools) that "A students become law professors, B students become judges and C students become millionaires." All of a sudden making a C doesn't sound as bad any more does it?

# Key #33: Remember that Lawyers Do Everything

The law and therefore lawyers touch every corner of every type of business or area of life. Law schools often push large law firms. Those are the companies that are able to come to your campus and recruit. It's easier and more accessible for career services to point you to resources regarding large firms. But, while large firms do hire a ton of lawyers, there are so many other options for you out there. All the focus on large firms during law school can make it easy for you to become disillusioned and lose focus because it seems like lawyers only go to work at large law firms.

If you came to law school to save the world, do your research and find firms, companies, or organizations that help save the world in the way you want to save the world. Every industry needs and utilizes lawyers. If you are interested in a certain industry, look into what it will take to get there. Maybe it's through a large firm but it's just as likely that it's through interning or volunteering for a person, company or organization in that area or arena. Working for free one or two summers has been known to lead people to the job of their dreams.

Lawyers are leading fortune 500 businesses, sports organizations, public service organizations, internet companies, etc. If you have an interest, explore how lawyers function in that area, because it may lead to the job you thought about getting when you applied to law school (or that you didn't even know existed before you began your research). Also, knowing your ultimate goal will help you stay focused during those times when all the hard work and long hours of law school seem unbearable. With a goal in mind, you'll know that law school is merely a stepping-stone and temporary hurdle to your ultimate destination and future success!

# Notes

www.ingramcontent.com/pod-product-compliance
Lightning Source LLC
Chambersburg PA
CBHW060632210326
41520CB00010B/1570